Making More

How Life Begins

KATHERINE ROY

NORTON YOUNG READERS
An Imprint of W. W. Norton & Company
Celebrating a Century of Independent Publishing

For Jackson and Tristan

Everywhere, all around you, life is making more.
Mammals and insects. Birds and reptiles. Trees and flowers.
Fish and frogs. Like food and water, like oxygen and
sunlight, reproduction is essential for life on Earth.

Making more looks different from species to species.
But the pattern stays the same: meet, merge, and create
something *new*. Most life that you see comes from this cycle.

Making more is the story of families,
of births and beginnings, of challenge
and chance. It is stunning. It is familiar.
It is life's greatest invention . . .

But *how* does life make more?
It begins with the instructions
inside of cells, known as genes . . .

Crossroads

one set of genes from the father

From the smallest ant to the tallest tree, every living creature is made to do two things: to survive and to make more of its kind. But most living things can't make copies of their bodies. To reproduce, they make copies of their *genes*.

Genes are the chemical instructions inside of cells that tell them what to do. They are why rabbits can only make more rabbits, and not more birds or beetles or bears. Genes are made of DNA, a long, spiraling molecule found in the cells of all living things. Just as we use our alphabet of 26 letters to make words and sentences, genes use the 4 chemical "letters" of DNA to make every part of every living organism. A complete set of genes is known as a genome.

All living creatures inherit genes from their parents. But in most plants and animals, it takes *two* sets of genes—one from each parent—to start a new life. The result is a baby that is a little bit different from its parents. It is also a little bit different from its siblings. This type of making more is called crossing, or sexual reproduction, and it's how most living things begin.

But how do the two sets of genes ever meet?

When it's time to make more, living things produce special cells called gametes that each carry a single set of genes. Gametes are made to travel, and they come in two sizes, large and small . . .

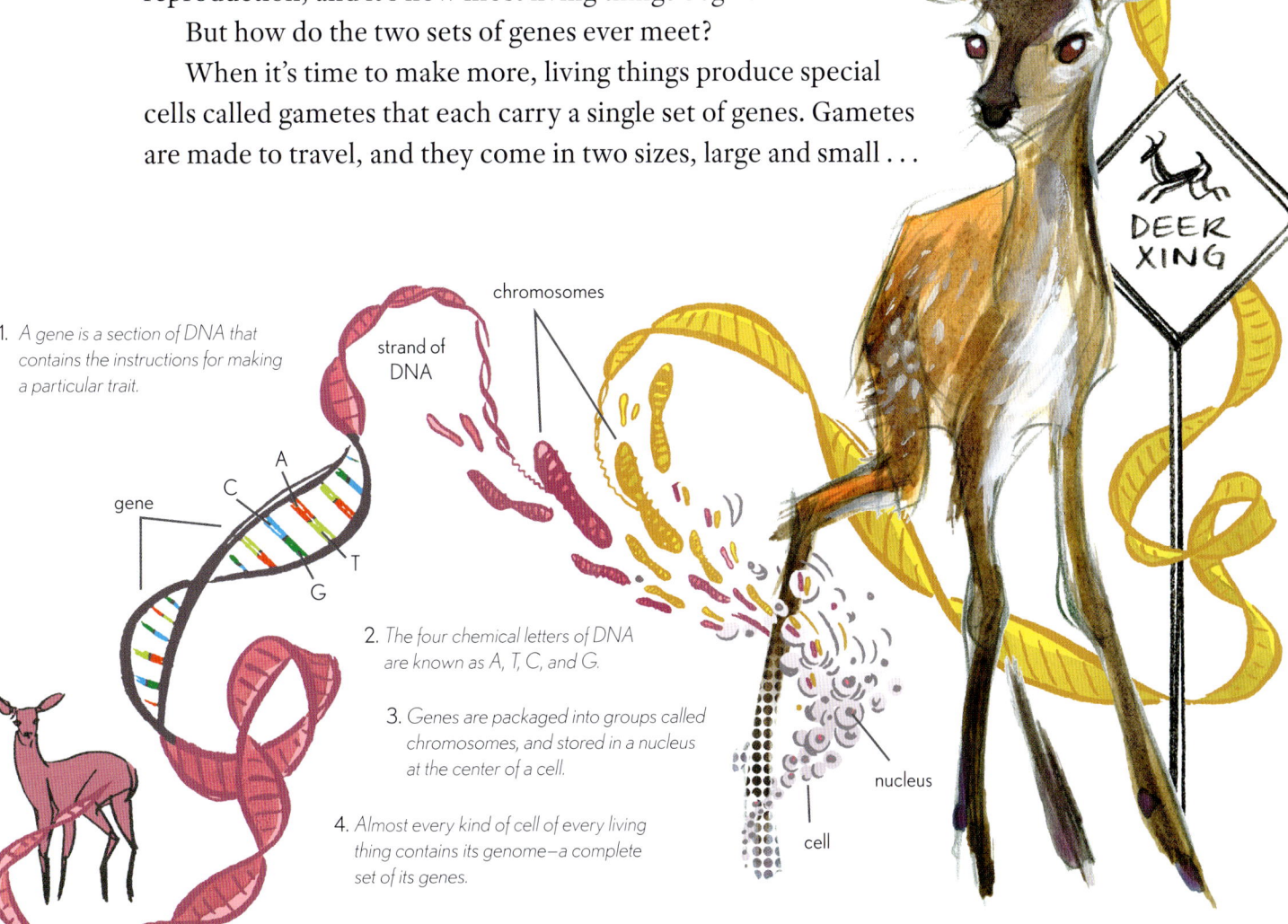

1. *A gene is a section of DNA that contains the instructions for making a particular trait.*

chromosomes

strand of DNA

gene

A
C
T
G

2. *The four chemical letters of DNA are known as A, T, C, and G.*

3. *Genes are packaged into groups called chromosomes, and stored in a nucleus at the center of a cell.*

4. *Almost every kind of cell of every living thing contains its genome–a complete set of its genes.*

nucleus

cell

one set of genes from the mother

baby with two sets of genes

Built for Life

TURTLE EGG CELL

nucleus

shell

yolk
(food supply)

Big, round, and packed with essential ingredients, an egg cell, or ovum, is the larger type of gamete. An animal that makes egg cells is called a female. Female animals produce egg cells inside of organs called ovaries. Plants also make large female gametes in the ovules of flowers and cones.

Egg cells are designed to sustain the start of a new life. They are larger than other kinds of cells so that they can divide again and again when it is time for them to grow. All animal egg cells have the same basic parts: a supply of food, a nucleus with one set of genes, and an outer membrane for protection. In flowering plants, the outer layer of an ovule will become the outside of a seed.

It takes days or weeks for a female's body to prepare her egg cells for their journey ahead. But once they are ready, they are too big to go far. It's time for egg cells to meet the other type of gamete, one that is much quicker and smaller in size . . .

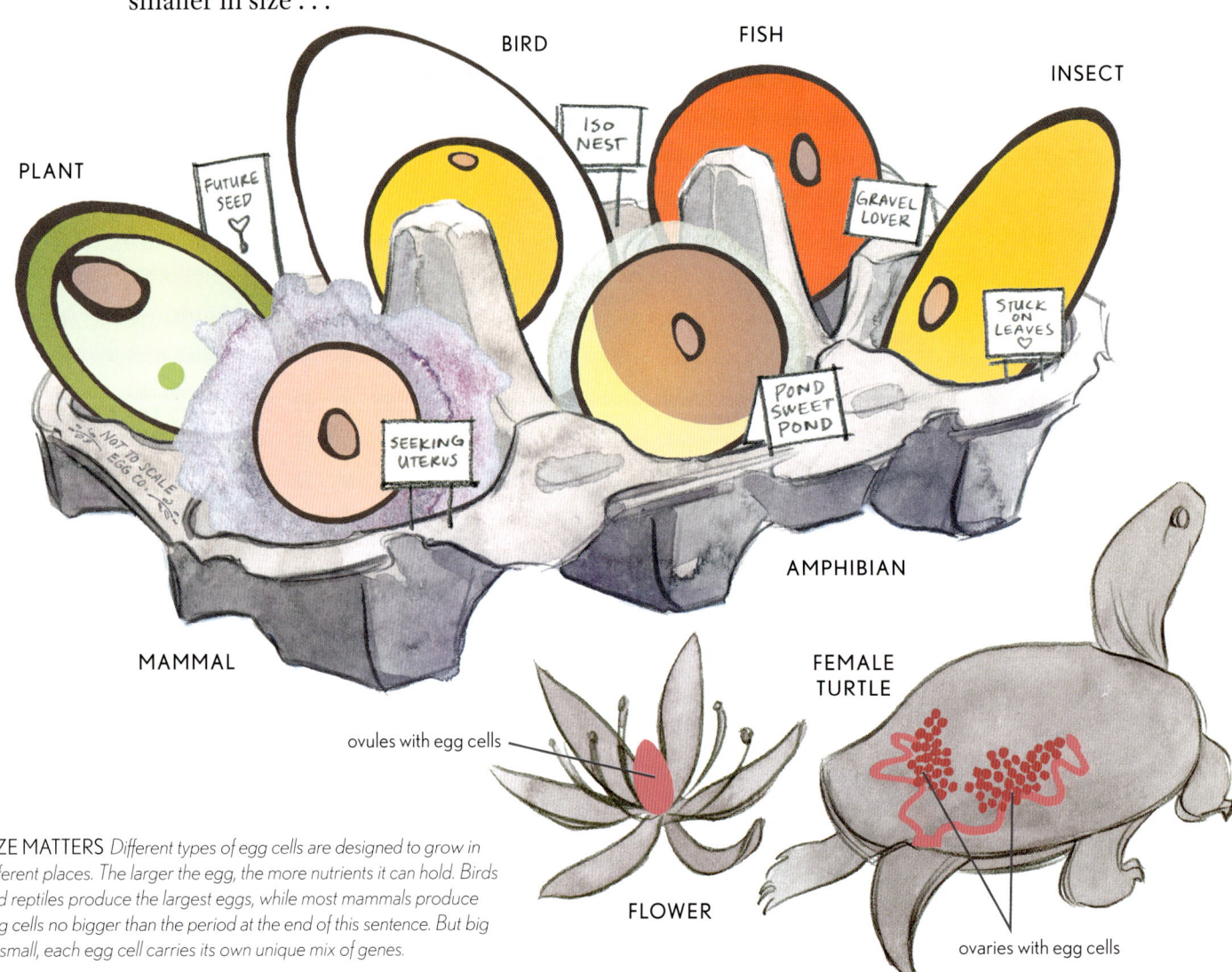

PLANT

FUTURE SEED

BIRD

ISO NEST

FISH

INSECT

GRAVEL LOVER

STUCK ON LEAVES

NOT TO SCALE EGG CO.

SEEKING UTERUS

POND SWEET POND

AMPHIBIAN

MAMMAL

ovules with egg cells

FLOWER

FEMALE TURTLE

ovaries with egg cells

SIZE MATTERS *Different types of egg cells are designed to grow in different places. The larger the egg, the more nutrients it can hold. Birds and reptiles produce the largest eggs, while most mammals produce egg cells no bigger than the period at the end of this sentence. But big or small, each egg cell carries its own unique mix of genes.*

Made to Move

Small, streamlined, and built for speed, a sperm cell is the smaller type of gamete. An animal that makes sperm cells is called a male. Male animals produce sperm inside of organs known as testes. Plants also produce sperm cells inside of pollen in flowers and cones.

Sperm cells are designed to find and fuse with—or fertilize— egg cells of the same species. This process results in a single cell with two sets of genes, and starts the growth of a brand new living thing. All animal sperm cells have the same basic parts: a supply of energy, a nucleus with one set of genes, and a cap made to fuse with an egg cell. Most sperm cells also have a whiplike tail that they use for swimming when outside of a male's body. In flowering plants, pollen grains are made to be carried to the ovules of neighboring plants.

With sperm cells ready and egg cells waiting, it's time for the two types of gametes to merge into a single cell. But how do two cells from two different bodies ever meet? First, males and females must find each other by putting out the right kind of signals . . .

tail

supply of energy

nucleus

cap

HUMMINGBIRD SPERM CELL

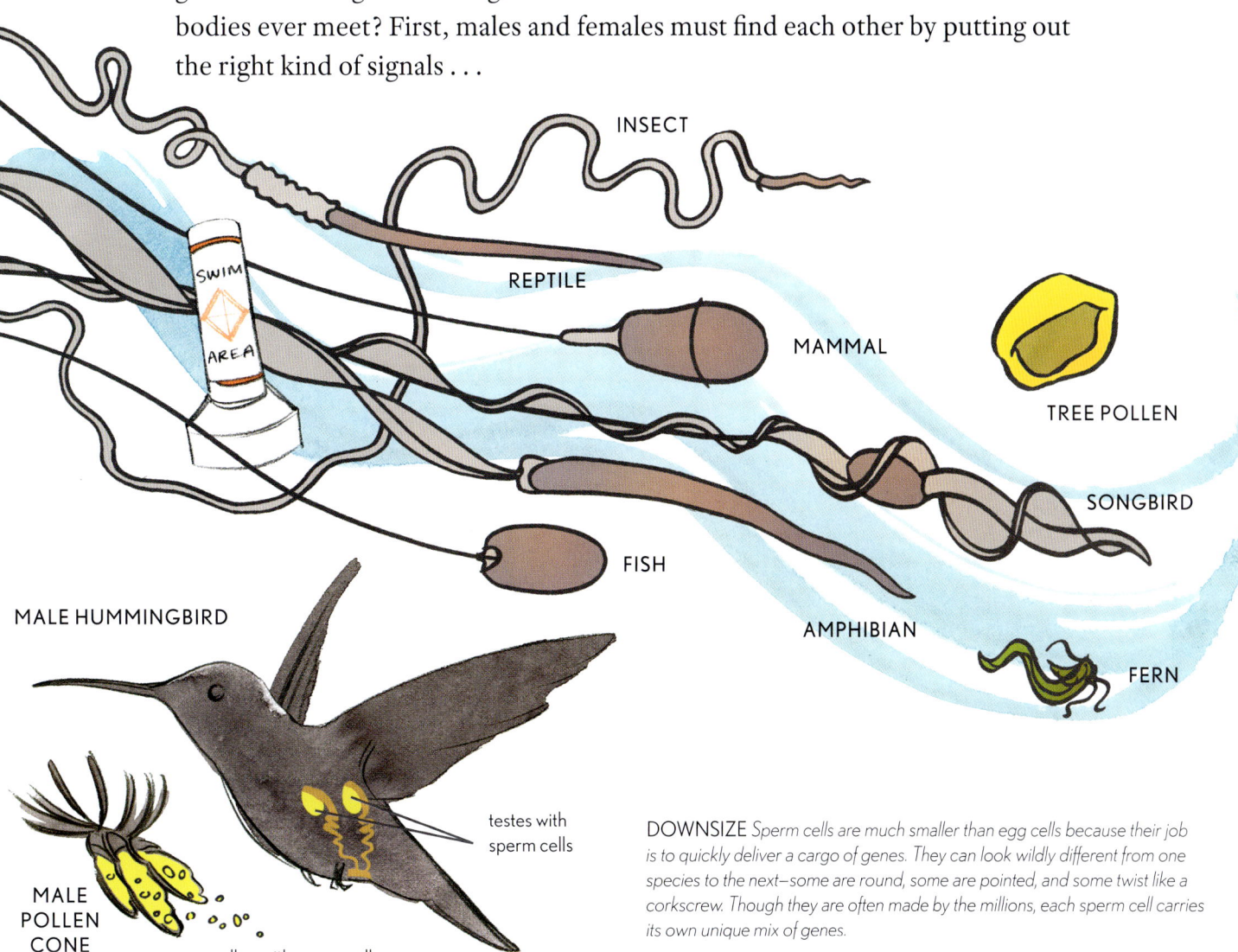

INSECT

REPTILE

MAMMAL

TREE POLLEN

SONGBIRD

FISH

AMPHIBIAN

FERN

MALE HUMMINGBIRD

SWIM AREA

testes with sperm cells

MALE POLLEN CONE

pollen with sperm cells

DOWNSIZE *Sperm cells are much smaller than egg cells because their job is to quickly deliver a cargo of genes. They can look wildly different from one species to the next—some are round, some are pointed, and some twist like a corkscrew. Though they are often made by the millions, each sperm cell carries its own unique mix of genes.*

Signal Bars

Longer days and warmer weather signal the start of spring. This is a season of sunlight, when plants grow and food is most abundant. Making more takes lots of energy, so the actions of living things are timed to match up with the extra meals. Chemical messages called hormones tell their bodies to get ready. Egg cells ripen, sperm cells mature, and males and females feel the need to attract a mate.

Courtship behaviors are unique to each species, but life has a few favorite ways of showing off. These signals—however strange—are life's way of shouting "Pick me! Pick me! I am healthy and ready to make more!" But pairing off is only the beginning of the task ahead. Just as cars can't get very far without a road, sperm cells and egg cells cannot meet without a path to travel between partners . . .

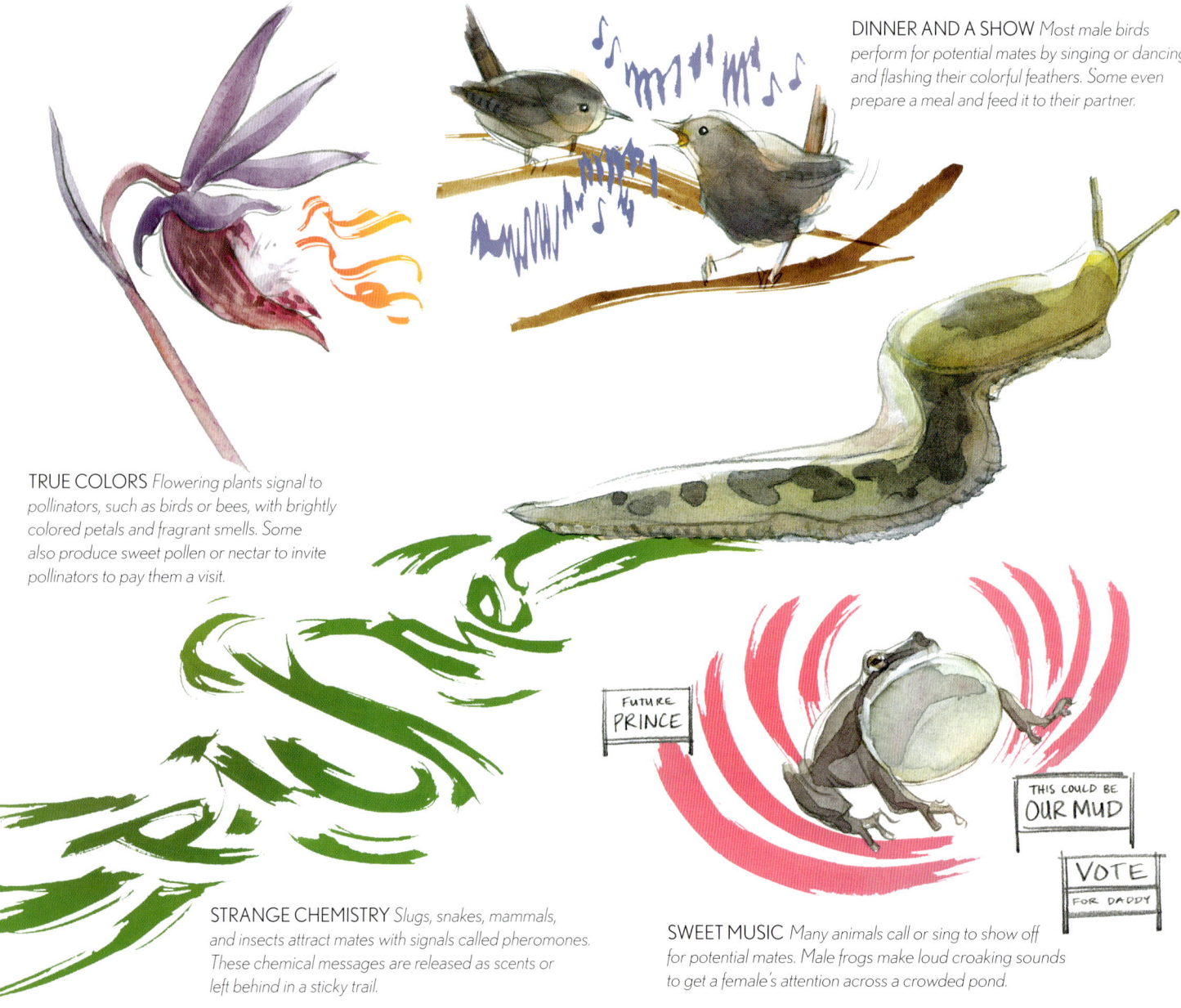

DINNER AND A SHOW *Most male birds perform for potential mates by singing or dancing and flashing their colorful feathers. Some even prepare a meal and feed it to their partner.*

TRUE COLORS *Flowering plants signal to pollinators, such as birds or bees, with brightly colored petals and fragrant smells. Some also produce sweet pollen or nectar to invite pollinators to pay them a visit.*

FUTURE PRINCE

THIS COULD BE OUR MUD

VOTE FOR DADDY

STRANGE CHEMISTRY *Slugs, snakes, mammals, and insects attract mates with signals called pheromones. These chemical messages are released as scents or left behind in a sticky trail.*

SWEET MUSIC *Many animals call or sing to show off for potential mates. Male frogs make loud croaking sounds to get a female's attention across a crowded pond.*

Outside Chance

For most fish and amphibians, the path for making more is called external fertilization. In this process, sperm cells fertilize egg cells while they are *outside* of their parents' bodies, in the surrounding water. A male's sperm cells leave his testes and exit his body through an opening called a vent. A female's egg cells leave her ovaries and exit her body through an opening, also called a vent. Partners bring their bodies close together and release their gametes into the water at the same time. Though most of the sperm cells and egg cells will be swept away or lost to predators, a few of the cells meet in the water. When they do, the two cells merge to become a single cell with two sets of genes. The fertilized egg is called a zygote, the beginning of a brand new, unique living thing. The water keeps the zygote moist as it begins to grow.

But how do gametes meet when partners live on dry land? It requires a different kind of path, one that keeps the traveling cells safe inside the female's body . . .

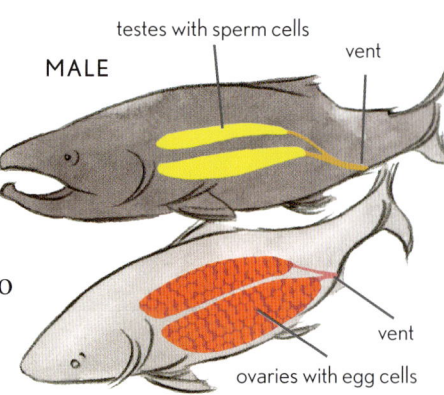

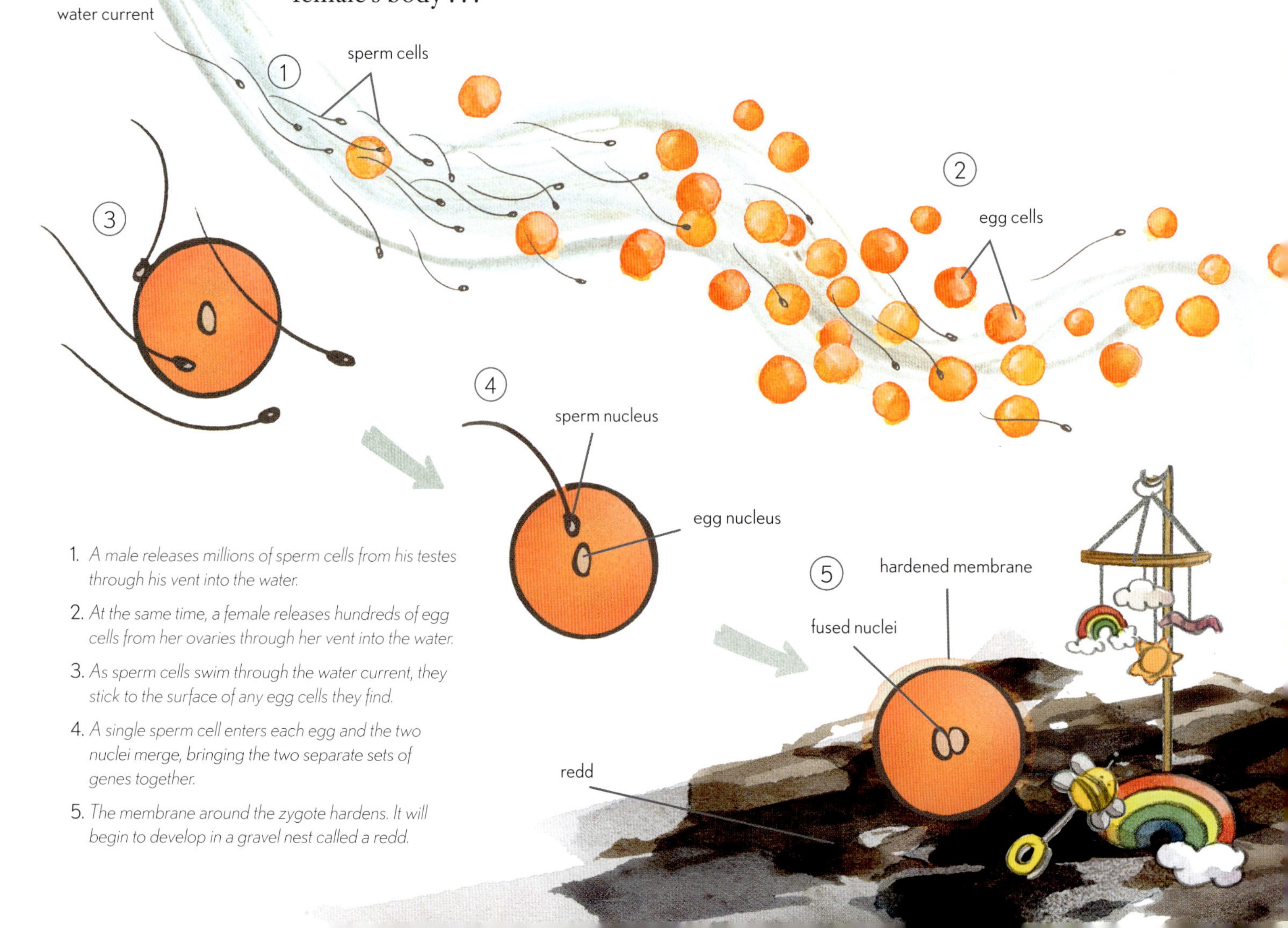

MALE — testes with sperm cells — vent

FEMALE — ovaries with egg cells — vent

water current

1 sperm cells

2 egg cells

3

4 sperm nucleus — egg nucleus

5 hardened membrane — fused nuclei

redd

1. *A male releases millions of sperm cells from his testes through his vent into the water.*

2. *At the same time, a female releases hundreds of egg cells from her ovaries through her vent into the water.*

3. *As sperm cells swim through the water current, they stick to the surface of any egg cells they find.*

4. *A single sperm cell enters each egg and the two nuclei merge, bringing the two separate sets of genes together.*

5. *The membrane around the zygote hardens. It will begin to develop in a gravel nest called a redd.*

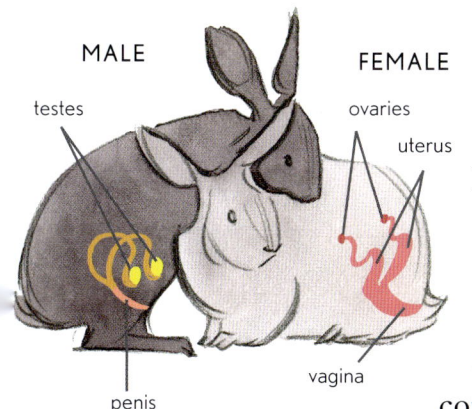

MALE

testes

FEMALE

ovaries

uterus

penis

vagina

Inside Story

For mammals, the path for making more is called internal fertilization. In this process, sperm cells fertilize egg cells while they are *inside* a female's body. Males have an organ called a penis that is designed for transferring sperm to a female. Females have a muscular tube called a vagina that connects to an internal organ called a uterus. To mate, a male releases his sperm cells through his penis into a female's vagina. This method of making more protects the egg cells, and ensures that fewer sperm and egg cells will be lost than with external fertilization.

Some female birds, reptiles, and insects can store sperm for future use. But in mammals, a sperm cell has only a few hours to find and fertilize an egg cell. When it does, the two cells merge and become a single fertilized cell, called a zygote. The zygote travels to its mother's uterus, where it can begin to grow.

But how do gametes meet when two partners are rooted in place? For most plants, making more takes a little help from their friends . . .

② egg cell

③ sperm cells

④ fertilized egg

⑤ zygote

FEMALE

ovary

uterine tube

uterus

ovary

uterine tube

1. *A male releases millions of sperm cells through his penis into a female's vagina.*

2. *At about the same time, a female's ovaries release one or many egg cells into her uterine tubes.*

3. *The sperm cells swim upward into the female's uterine tubes. There, some of the sperm cells find egg cells and stick to their surface.*

4. *A single sperm enters each egg cell, and the two nuclei merge.*

5. *The zygotes continue downward to the uterus. Some mammals, such as rabbits, have two uteruses.*

uterus

vagina

testes

MALE

①

sperm cells

sperm cells

penis

Long-Distance Relationship

For most plants, the path for making more depends on a delivery service. Though some species can pollinate themselves or send out stems called runners that make new plants, most need to cross with other plants to make new offspring. Seed-producing plants make pollen and egg cells in temporary structures such as flowers or cones. Then the wind, water, or a nearby animal carries the pollen to the ovules of other plants. As a result, plant parents can make more without ever needing to meet!

ovules with egg cells (female)

anther with pollen (male)

Some plants, like ferns, begin to grow just after fertilization. Others, like flowering plants, first develop inside a protective shell, or seed. But plants aren't the only ones to get their start inside a shell. In birds and reptiles, a special gland in the females makes it possible to bring what's inside out . . .

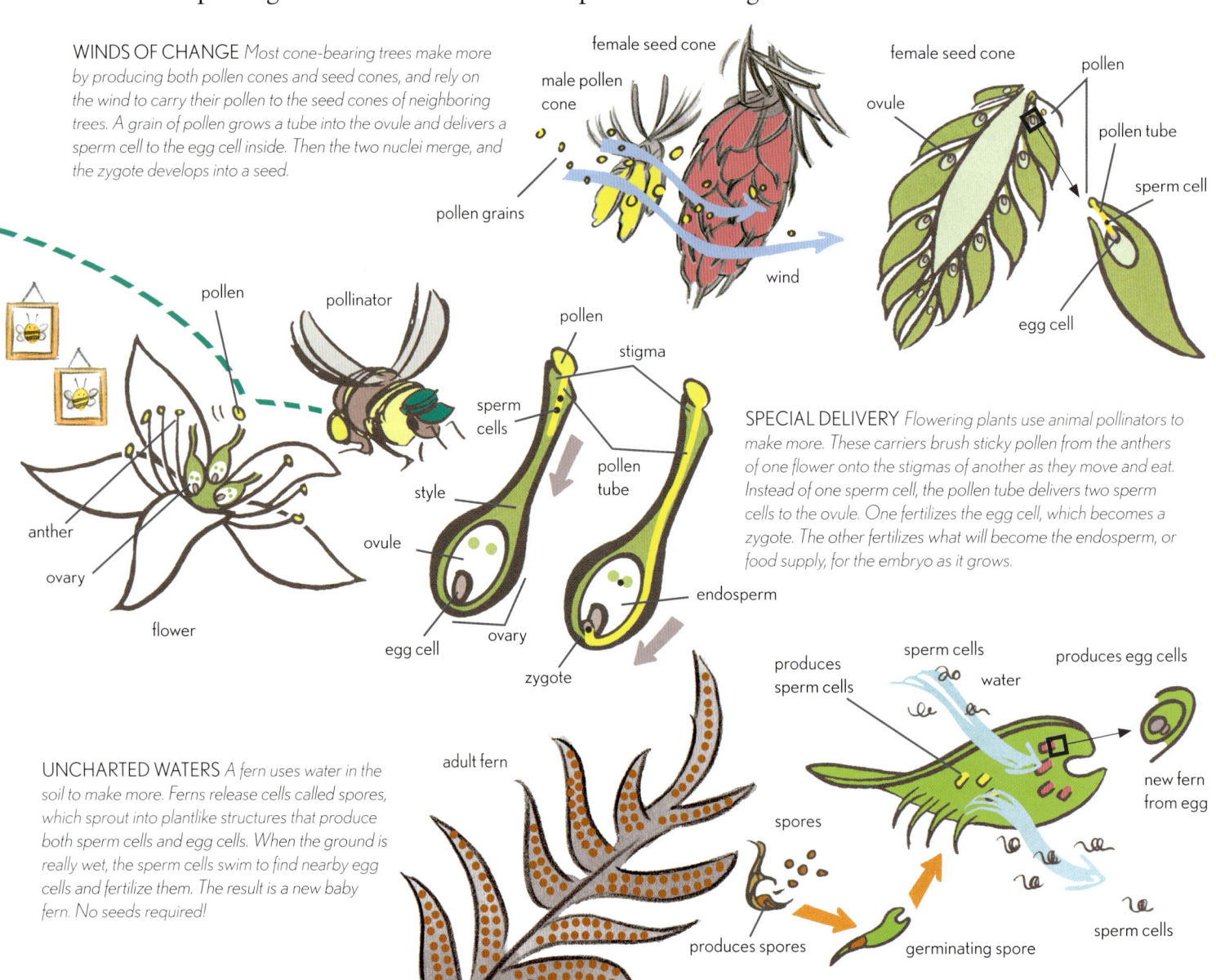

WINDS OF CHANGE *Most cone-bearing trees make more by producing both pollen cones and seed cones, and rely on the wind to carry their pollen to the seed cones of neighboring trees. A grain of pollen grows a tube into the ovule and delivers a sperm cell to the egg cell inside. Then the two nuclei merge, and the zygote develops into a seed.*

female seed cone
male pollen cone
pollen grains
wind

female seed cone
ovule
pollen
pollen tube
sperm cell
egg cell

pollen
pollinator

anther
ovary
flower

pollen
stigma
sperm cells
style
ovule
pollen tube
egg cell
ovary
zygote
endosperm

SPECIAL DELIVERY *Flowering plants use animal pollinators to make more. These carriers brush sticky pollen from the anthers of one flower onto the stigmas of another as they move and eat. Instead of one sperm cell, the pollen tube delivers two sperm cells to the ovule. One fertilizes the egg cell, which becomes a zygote. The other fertilizes what will become the endosperm, or food supply, for the embryo as it grows.*

UNCHARTED WATERS *A fern uses water in the soil to make more. Ferns release cells called spores, which sprout into plantlike structures that produce both sperm cells and egg cells. When the ground is really wet, the sperm cells swim to find nearby egg cells and fertilize them. The result is a new baby fern. No seeds required!*

adult fern
produces sperm cells
sperm cells
water
produces egg cells
new fern from egg
spores
produces spores
germinating spore
sperm cells

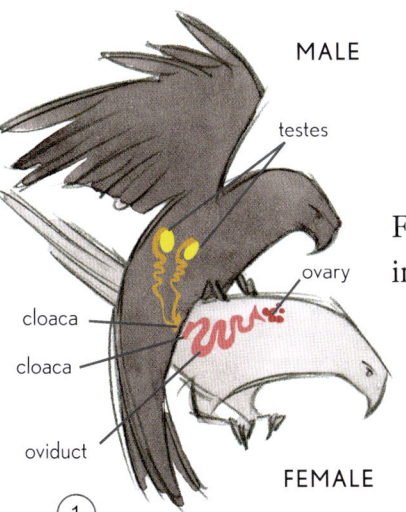

MALE

testes

ovary

cloaca

cloaca

oviduct

① FEMALE

Inside Out

For birds and reptiles, the path for making more is also called internal fertilization. As in mammals, sperm and egg cells meet and merge *inside* a female. Then her body forms a shell around each zygote after fertilization. In all birds and most reptiles, the finished egg exits her body to develop *outside* in the world.

All birds and reptiles have a cloaca, a single opening used for reproduction and waste. To mate, a male transfers his sperm cells to a female through this opening. Her body stores the sperm cells until she is ready to lay new eggs. Once a sperm cell finds and fertilizes an egg cell, the new zygote travels down through its mother's oviduct. Along the way it is packaged with water and nutrients, and then sealed inside a tough outer shell. Most reptiles lay their eggs all at once, but birds lay one egg at a time until their clutch of eggs is complete.

Whether animal or plant, made inside or out, at last the single-celled zygote begins to divide. It is now called an embryo. But before it can emerge as a new baby, it needs a safe place to develop and grow . . .

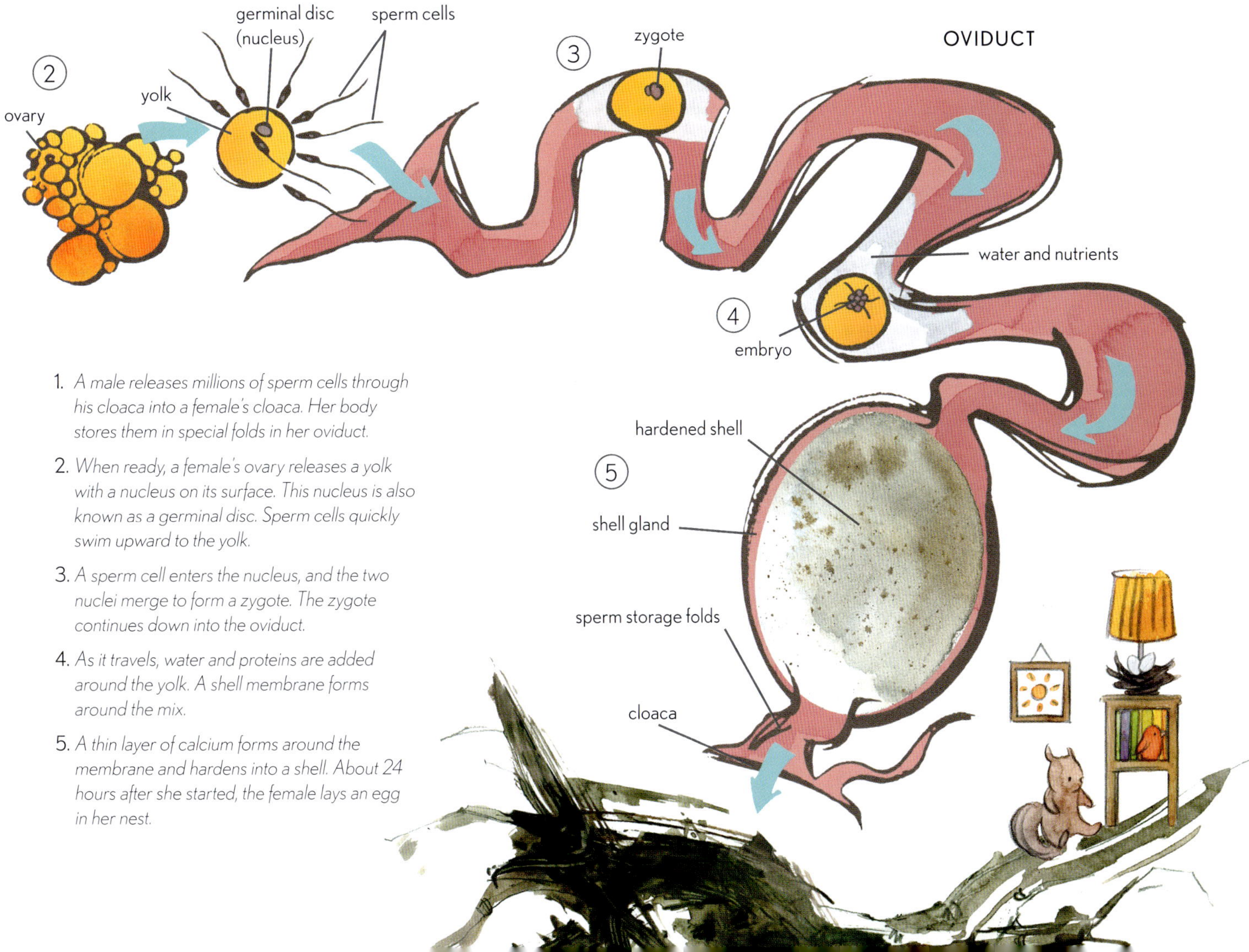

germinal disc (nucleus)   sperm cells

② yolk

ovary

③ zygote   OVIDUCT

water and nutrients

④ embryo

hardened shell

⑤ shell gland

sperm storage folds

cloaca

1. *A male releases millions of sperm cells through his cloaca into a female's cloaca. Her body stores them in special folds in her oviduct.*

2. *When ready, a female's ovary releases a yolk with a nucleus on its surface. This nucleus is also known as a germinal disc. Sperm cells quickly swim upward to the yolk.*

3. *A sperm cell enters the nucleus, and the two nuclei merge to form a zygote. The zygote continues down into the oviduct.*

4. *As it travels, water and proteins are added around the yolk. A shell membrane forms around the mix.*

5. *A thin layer of calcium forms around the membrane and hardens into a shell. About 24 hours after she started, the female lays an egg in her nest.*

The Great Divide

Fish and amphibians get their start in ponds, oceans, rivers, and streams. To grow, an embryo's cells divide, and divide again, over and over and over. Soon there are thousands—then millions and billions—of cells, each with a job to do and a place to be, according to its genes. Some cells team up to build eyes or gills, while others build a spine or a heart. The yolk provides an embryo with food as it develops. The surrounding water keeps the embryo moist, and delivers oxygen while carrying off waste.

water brings oxygen

jelly coating

zygote

yolk

water carries away waste

The amount of time it takes for an embryo to hatch is determined by the water temperature and the instructions in its genes. Some species need several months to grow. Others need just a few days. Most fish and amphibians emerge from their eggs as larva, an immature stage between hatching and adulthood. Fish spend their lives in the water, but most amphibians leave for land after changing into their final adult form.

But how does an embryo develop on dry land? Some species bring the water with them . . .

AMPHIBIAN EMBRYO

2-celled stage

4-celled stage

8-celled stage

blastula

gastrula

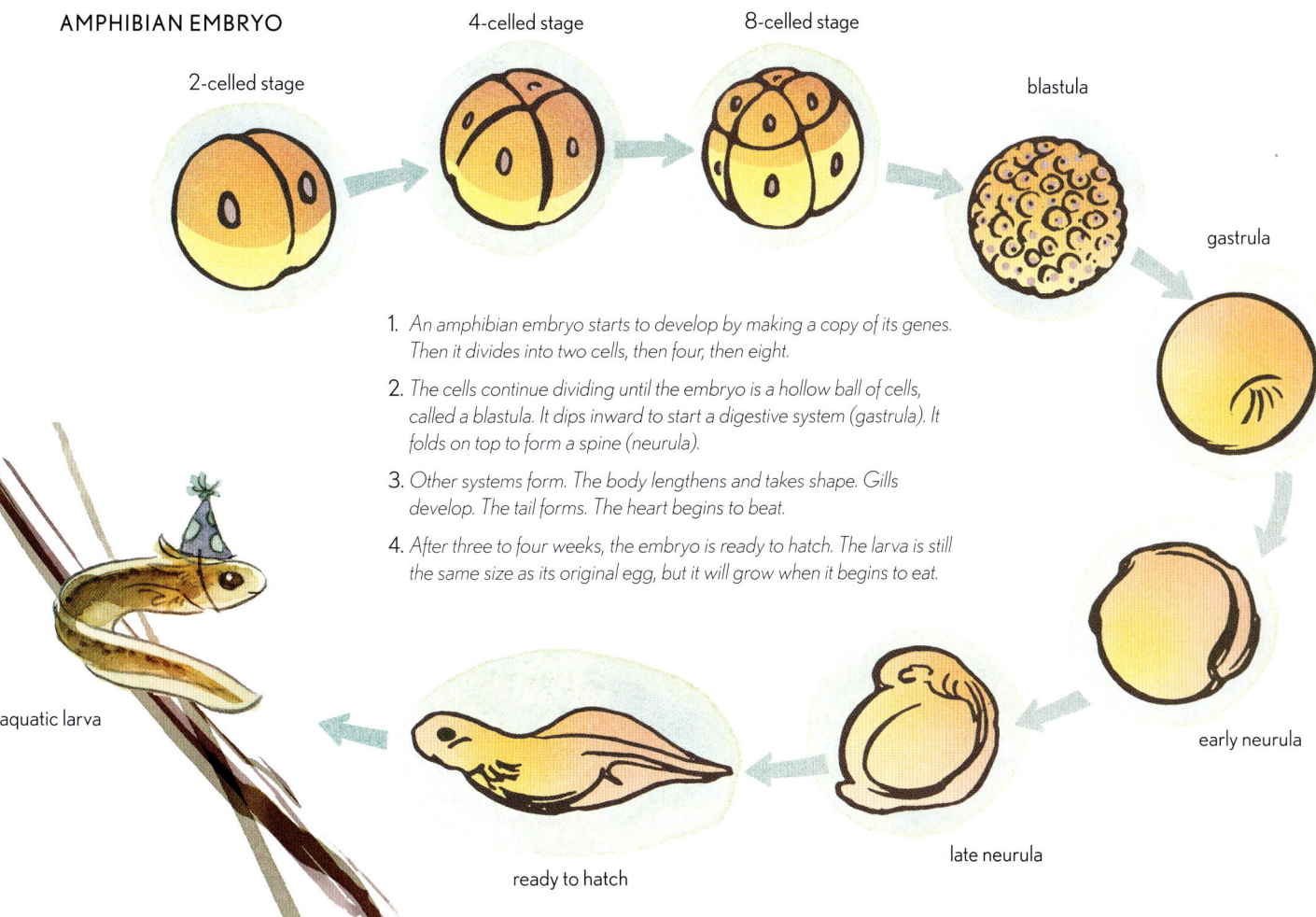

1. *An amphibian embryo starts to develop by making a copy of its genes. Then it divides into two cells, then four, then eight.*

2. *The cells continue dividing until the embryo is a hollow ball of cells, called a blastula. It dips inward to start a digestive system (gastrula). It folds on top to form a spine (neurula).*

3. *Other systems form. The body lengthens and takes shape. Gills develop. The tail forms. The heart begins to beat.*

4. *After three to four weeks, the embryo is ready to hatch. The larva is still the same size as its original egg, but it will grow when it begins to eat.*

aquatic larva

ready to hatch

late neurula

early neurula

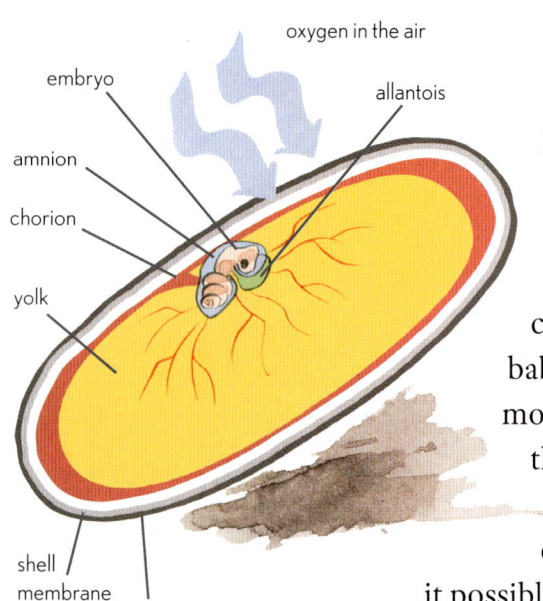

AMNIOTIC EGG

- oxygen in the air
- embryo
- allantois
- amnion
- chorion
- yolk
- shell membrane
- shell

Pond for One

Birds and reptiles spend their whole lives on land, but they still begin life in the water. Instead of starting in an open stream, their shells keep them sealed inside a tiny pond for one. As an embryo develops, some cells become the growing baby. Other cells become the baby's life support system. The shell membrane holds in moisture, and a fluid-filled sac called the amnion keeps the embryo safe. A membrane called the chorion provides the embryo with oxygen, and another called the allantois stores waste. These structures make it possible for an embryo to grow on land without drying out.

All birds need heat to develop, but reptiles develop at cooler temperatures. As the embryo uses up its food supply in the yolk, the yolk shrinks and the embryo grows, taking up more and more space inside of its shell. When an embryo is out of room and nearly out of food, it is time to hatch. After hatching, most baby birds are fed by their parents for days or weeks, while baby reptiles find food on their own.

But eggshells are just one kind of cradle for an embryo on land. Most plants begin their development inside the tough case of a seed . . .

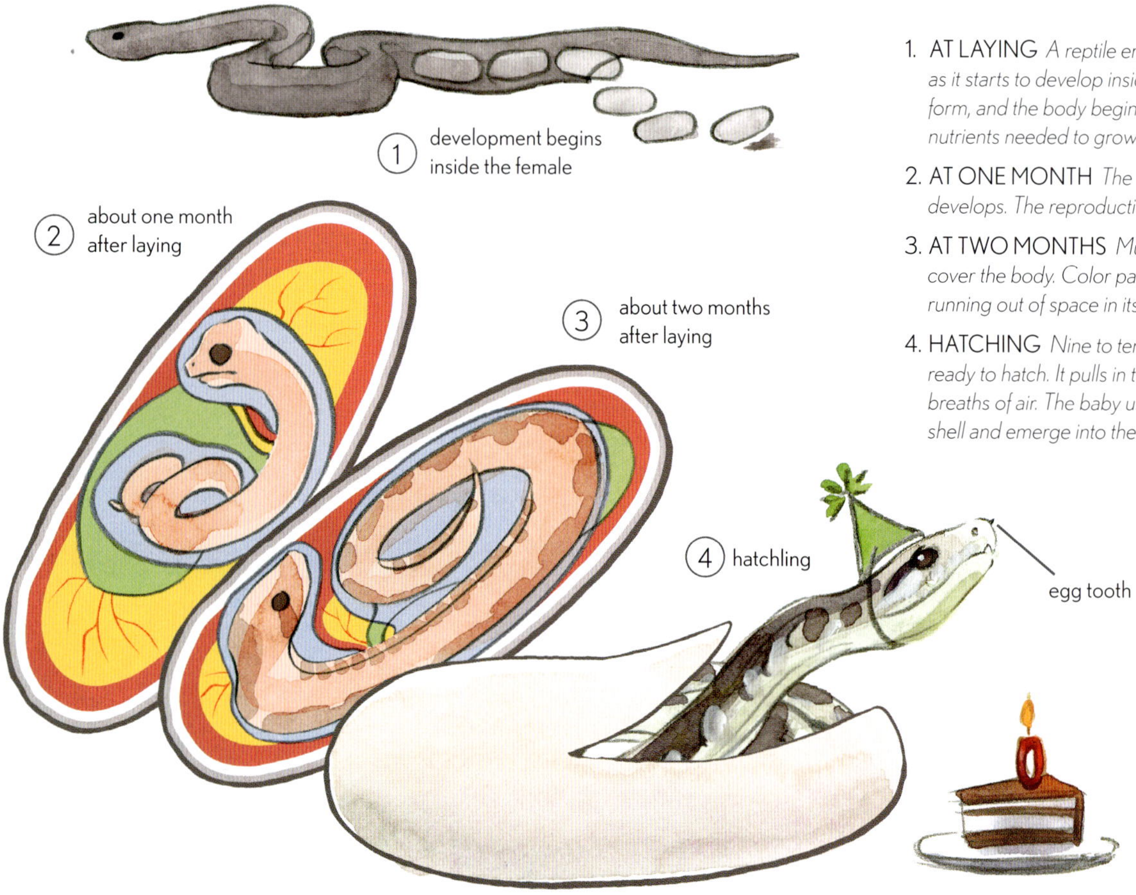

① development begins inside the female

② about one month after laying

③ about two months after laying

④ hatchling

egg tooth

1. **AT LAYING** *A reptile embryo divides, folds, and lengthens as it starts to develop inside of its shell. The eyes and nose form, and the body begins to coil. The yolk supplies the nutrients needed to grow.*

2. **AT ONE MONTH** *The eyes and nose darken. The tongue develops. The reproductive organs take shape.*

3. **AT TWO MONTHS** *Muscles develop. Scales form and cover the body. Color patterns start to appear. The embryo is running out of space in its shell.*

4. **HATCHING** *Nine to ten weeks after laying, the embryo is ready to hatch. It pulls in the remaining yolk and takes its first breaths of air. The baby uses its egg tooth to break through its shell and emerge into the world.*

Ground Breaking

A new plant gets its start while it is still attached to its parent plant. But instead of growing in a watery sac, most plant embryos develop in a protected seed. To grow, some cells team up to build a root, while other cells become a shoot with one or two leaves, called cotyledons. Still other cells fill up with a store of starchy nutrients supplied by the parent plant. A protective shell, called a seed coat, forms around an embryo and its food supply. The surrounding ovary develops into either a dried pod or a juicy fruit.

Fruits and pods are made to travel so that the seeds inside can survive the journey to new soil. Some fly. Some float. Some stick to feathers or fur. And some are so delicious that they're carried off to be eaten. Once development is done, a seed needs several weeks or months to rest before it is ready to sprout. It germinates as a new baby plant when the conditions outside are just right.

But plants aren't the only parents that directly feed their embryos as they grow . . .

MATURE OAK EMBRYO

radicle (early root)

hypocotyl (early shoot)

seed coat

cotyledons (early leaves)

cupule

① parent oak tree

ovary

embryo

suspensor

ovule

② globular stage

embryo

③ heart stage

cotyledon

radicle

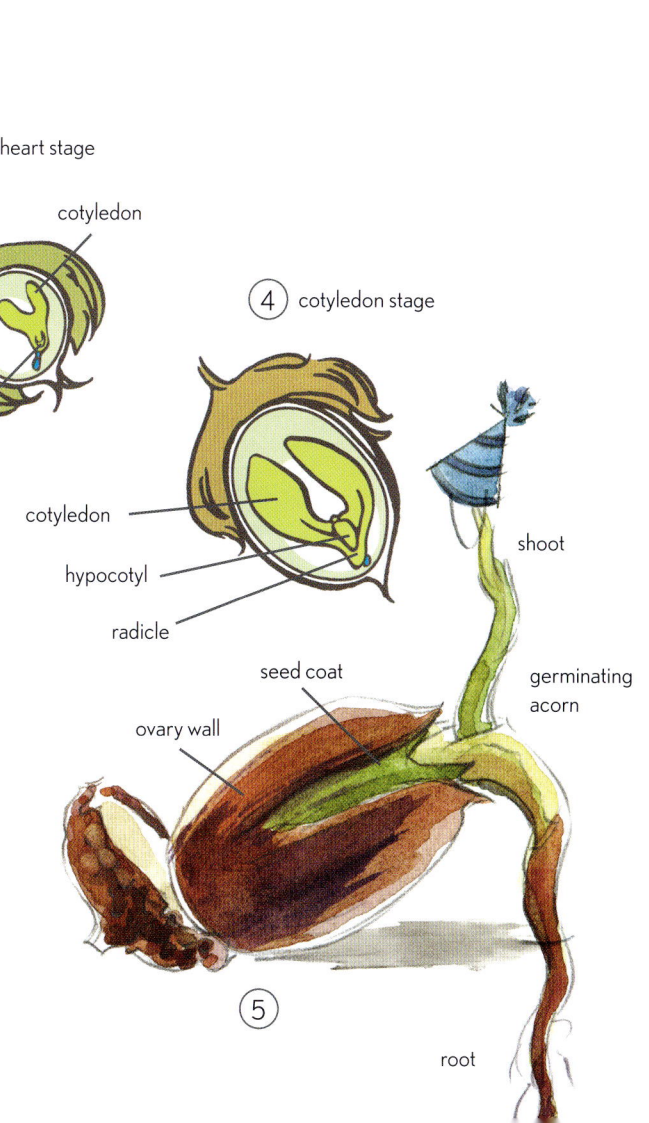

④ cotyledon stage

cotyledon

hypocotyl

radicle

seed coat

ovary wall

shoot

germinating acorn

root

⑤

1. An oak embryo starts to develop by making a copy of its genes. Then it divides into two cells. The smaller cell will become the embryo. The larger cell will become a structure that keeps the embryo in place (suspensor).

2. The cells continue to divide as the embryo grows inside the ovule (globular stage).

3. The early root forms (radicle) and the early leaves (cotyledons) start to take shape (heart stage).

4. The early shoot (hypocotyl) forms. The cotyledons absorb more and more nutrients as the embryo fills the seed (cotyledon stage).

5. After about 12 months, an oak embryo is mature. The ovule forms into a seed coat. The ovary dries and becomes a hard pod. The acorn rests before sprouting into a new oak seedling.

MAMMAL EMBRYO

amniotic sac

placenta

uterus

umbilical cord

Room to Grow

Mammals, too, get their start in a body of water. But instead of in a shell or a stream, they float in a private pool inside their mother. After fertilization, an embryo travels to its mother's uterus. The embryo then attaches to the soft lining of the uterus to continue to grow. Some cells become the baby, while other cells become the baby's life support system. The amniotic sac holds fluid and expands like a balloon around an embryo as it grows. An organ called a placenta delivers food and oxygen from the mother and removes waste through a twisty tube called the umbilical cord.

Most large mammals have one or two offspring at a time. Smaller mammals can have litters of four to twelve or more. A mother's uterus stretches bigger and bigger as her passengers grow larger. After several weeks or months of development, the babies are ready to eat and breathe on their own. Muscles in the mother's uterus contract and squeeze, pushing each baby down and out of her vagina in a process called birth. She will feed her newborns milk from special glands on her torso until they are ready to find food on their own . . .

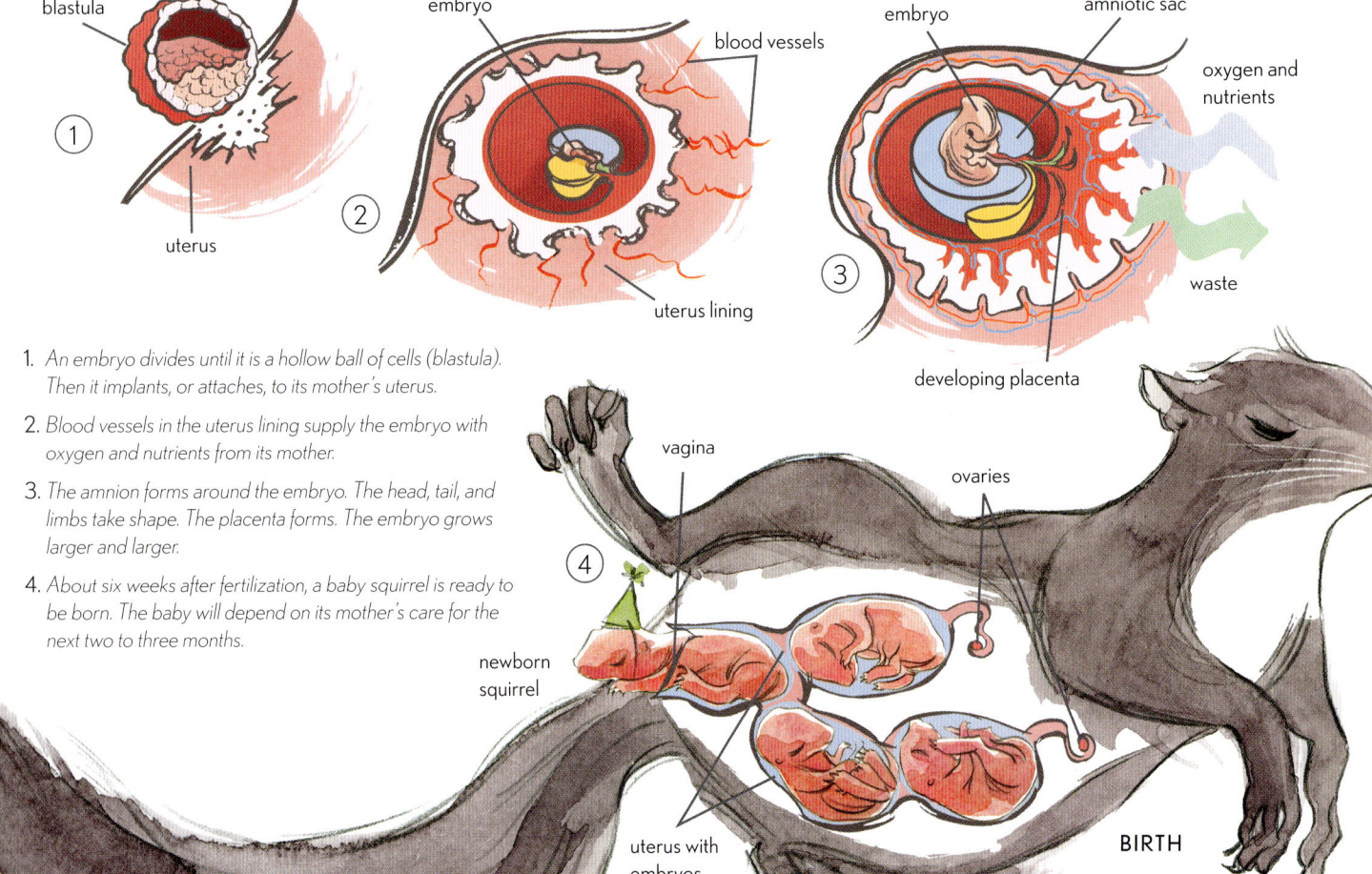

blastula

uterus

①

embryo

blood vessels

②

uterus lining

embryo

amniotic sac

oxygen and nutrients

waste

③

developing placenta

1. *An embryo divides until it is a hollow ball of cells (blastula). Then it implants, or attaches, to its mother's uterus.*

2. *Blood vessels in the uterus lining supply the embryo with oxygen and nutrients from its mother.*

3. *The amnion forms around the embryo. The head, tail, and limbs take shape. The placenta forms. The embryo grows larger and larger.*

4. *About six weeks after fertilization, a baby squirrel is ready to be born. The baby will depend on its mother's care for the next two to three months.*

④

vagina

ovaries

newborn squirrel

uterus with embryos

BIRTH

But Not So Fast!

Even after this incredible process—meeting, merging, and building new bodies—making more is just the beginning. Though parents are able to have lots of offspring, resources are limited. Living things must struggle to compete for food, water, and space. Only a tiny fraction of the eggs that are laid, the babies that are born, and the seeds that are scattered will survive long enough to become adults. The rest will die from disaster, disease, starvation, or be eaten by predators.

But in spite of these odds, some offspring *do* make it, and grow up to have babies of their own. Their success depends in part on their particular mix of genes, because no two individuals are exactly the same . . .

DISASTER *Floods, fires, freezing weather, and chance accidents are a common cause of death for living things. Even the best mix of genes can't save an offspring from bad luck, like leaping onto a broken branch.*

DISEASE *Parasites and diseases are common enemies for plants and animals. Some offspring might inherit genes that help them recover from sickness quickly, while others struggle to survive the same illness.*

PREDATORS *Prey animals are well adapted at escaping their predators, but some offspring might be quicker than others. Not all predators are meat eaters. Seed predators hunt and damage seeds.*

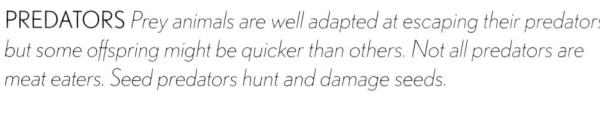

Change Maker

Remember how crossing two sets of genes makes a baby that is a little bit different from its parents? This might not seem important, but it is fundamental to life as we know it. No two squirrels or butterflies are exactly alike because they each inherit a unique mix of genes. And some genes produce traits that are more helpful in a particular environment. Genes that make an individual better able to survive and reproduce will spread. Over time, a population can adapt to better fit its environment.

Not *all* living things use crossing to make more. Bacteria copy their DNA and then divide into two new identical daughter cells. Some plants and animals are exclusively female, and produce eggs and seeds with nearly the same genes as their own. This type of making more is called cloning, or asexual reproduction, and it can quickly make far more offspring than crossing. Yet populations of clones are always at risk of going extinct. Without a way to shuffle genes and combine genetic changes, called mutations, it's hard to adapt in an ever-changing world . . .

CROSSING

mother

father

gene without
disease resistance

gene with disease
resistance

disease

male and female offspring

CLONING

mother plant

gene without
poison resistance

weed killer

all female offspring

WORLD OF DIFFERENCE *Crossing results in individuals that are a little bit different from each other. This variation between offspring comes from the different mix of genes inherited from two different parents. Though it takes more energy for a female butterfly to produce young by crossing, the effort is worthwhile because her offspring will have different traits. A gene that gives an offspring resistance to a disease might help it survive, and then that gene might get passed on to their offspring in turn.*

SAME AS ALWAYS *Cloning results in individuals that are all the same as one another. Changes in DNA called mutations are the only source of variation between a parent and its offspring. Dandelions are one of the most common clones—every plant is a female and can produce young alone. But with so few differences between them, an entire family might be defenseless against the same weed killer. No genes will be passed on, and the population will be lost.*

Generation Next

Planet Earth is a place of constant change. Ecosystems shift, food webs collapse, disasters arise, and new diseases emerge. Predators alter the population of their prey just by hunting. To survive, a species must be able to adapt and change to keep up with these many pressures. Thanks to the differences, or variations, that come from genetic mutations and crossing, life *can* change one generation at a time. With many generations of selection and pressure, what began as one species can gradually change, or evolve, into many. The millions of species alive today are all connected by this process of evolution. Our genes reveal a shared history, dating back to the earliest life on Earth. It is an endless, relentless, astonishing race that transformed ancient reptiles into birds and pond algae into orchids. The result is biodiversity, the rich variety of living things that call our planet home.

Crossing doesn't make life easy—it is often at odds with survival itself. But it persists because it enables life to change. In the end, individuals die. But life can go on and on by making more.

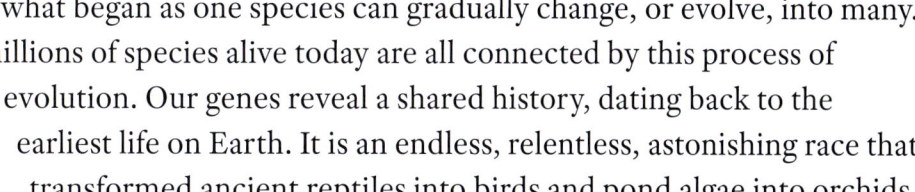

All around you, everywhere, life is making *more*. *More* mammals and insects. *More* birds and reptiles. *More* trees and flowers. *More* fish and frogs. One generation creates another. Without this cycle, life would cease.

Making more connects all species, and shapes the species yet to be. From common genes come new beginnings, different than what came before.

It is the story of life on Earth.

Making more is the story of heritage,
of effort and instinct, of survival and
change. It is rich. It is wild.
It is a story we share . . .

Key Terms

Amniotic egg—An egg that contains specialized membranes for feeding, protecting, and exchanging gas inside of a shell. The different membranes are called the amnion, the allantois, the chorion, and the shell membrane. These structures create a tiny private pond that make it possible for an embryo to develop on land instead of in the water.

Asexual reproduction—See **Cloning**.

Biodiversity—The variety of living things in a habitat or ecosystem. Biodiversity is the result of evolution through the process of natural selection.

Birth—The process by which the muscles in a mother's uterus contract and squeeze to push a baby down and out of her body. A "birthday" is the anniversary of the day a baby was born.

Cell—The basic building block of all living things. A cell has three main parts: an outer membrane, a mass of cytoplasm, and a nucleus. All organisms begin life as a single cell, and almost every kind of cell contains an organism's complete set of genes.

Chromosome—A package of tightly coiled DNA that is stored in the nucleus of a cell. Chromosomes are made up of genes, which determine the physical traits of an organism. The number of chromosomes in "two sets" of genes is different for each species. Fruit flies have 8 chromosomes, butterflies have 380, deer have 70, and humans have 46—or two sets of 23. Having more or less chromosomes does not make a species bigger or smaller, or more or less intelligent.

Cloning—The process of reproduction from the genes of just one parent without any exchange of gametes. This results in offspring that are genetically the same as their parent except for changes to DNA called mutations. Many plants, insects, and invertebrates are capable of cloning.

Crossing—The process of reproduction from the genes of two different parents by fusing a male gamete and a female gamete during fertilization. This results in offspring that are a little bit different from their parents. Crossing is how most known living things reproduce.

DNA—Deoxyribonucleic acid is a long, spiraling molecule that carries the instructions for the development and function of all living things. It is composed of four chemical compounds, known by the letters A, T, C, and G, which stand for adenine (A), thymine (T), cytosine (C), and guanine (G).

Egg cell—The larger type of gamete, or reproductive cell. An egg cell is also called an ovum. Egg cells are made by female animals in organs called ovaries. In plants, egg cells are made in the ovules of flowers and cones. Each egg cell carries a single set of genes and is designed to fuse with a sperm cell during fertilization to start a new life.

Embryo—A plant or animal organism in an early stage of development.

Evolution—The change in traits from one generation to the next that makes it possible for a population to adapt to its environment. Evolution relies on the process of natural selection and demonstrates that the species alive today are the descendants of other ancestral species.

External fertilization—Fertilization that takes place outside of the body of an organism, such as in fish and amphibians.

Fertilization—The process of a sperm cell fusing with an egg cell during sexual reproduction. It results in a single cell with two sets of genes, and starts the growth of a brand new living thing.

List of Species, in Order of Appearance

American Robin (*Turdus migratorius*)
Racer Snake (*Coluber constrictor*)
Two-Spotted Lady Beetle (*Adalia bipunctata*)
Black-Tailed Deer (*Odocoileus hemionus*)
Western Pond Turtle (*Actinemys marmorata*)
Common Camas (*Camassia quamash*)
Rufous Hummingbird (*Selasphorus rufus*)
Douglas Fir (*Pseudotsuga menziesii*)
Fairy Slipper Orchid (*Calypso bulbosa*)
Pacific Wren (*Troglodytes pacificus*)
Pacific Banana Slug (*Ariolimax columbianus*)
Pacific Chorus Frog (*Pseudacris regilla*)
Coastal Rainbow Trout (*Oncorhynchus mykiss*)
Brush Rabbit (*Sylvilagus bachmani*)

Pacific Blackberry (*Rubus ursinus*)
Fuzzy-Horned Bumblebee (*Bombus mixtus*)
Western Sword Fern (*Polystichum munitum*)
Red-Tailed Hawk (*Buteo jamaicensis*)
Rough-Skinned Newt (*Taricha granulosa*)
Gopher Snake (*Pituophis catenifer*)
White Oak (*Quercus garryana*)
Western Gray Squirrel (*Sciurus griseus*)
Anise Swallowtail (*Papilio zelicaon*)
Common Dandelion (*Taraxacum officinale*)
Coyote (*Canis latrans*)
Painted Turtle (*Chrysemys picta*)
Chinook Salmon (*Oncorhynchus tshawytscha*)
Steller's Jay (*Cyanocitta stelleri*)

Gamete—The special reproductive cells that living organisms produce and which carry a single set of genes. Female gametes are called egg cells, and male gametes are called sperm cells. Egg cells and sperm cells are designed to fuse together during the process of fertilization.

Genes—The chemical instructions inside of cells that tell them what to do. Genes are made of DNA and packaged into chromosomes that are stored in the nucleus of a cell. Genes are passed from parent to offspring through the process of reproduction, and make it possible for offspring to inherit a particular trait or feature.

Germination—The process of a seed or spore sprouting into a new plant after a period of rest.

Internal fertilization—Fertilization that takes place inside the body of an organism, such as in birds, reptiles, mammals, and most insects.

Mutation—A change in the DNA sequence of a gene. Mutations are the ultimate source of all genetic variation.

Nucleus (plural, nuclei)—The large, membrane-bound structure found in cells that contains an organism's genes in the form of chromosomes. During fertilization, the nucleus in an egg cell fuses with the nucleus from a sperm cell to produce a single-celled zygote with two sets of genes.

Ovary—In female animals, the organ that produces egg cells. In flowering plants, the structure that contains the ovules, where egg cells are produced.

Oviduct—The tube that connects an ovary to the shell gland in a female bird or reptile.

Ovule—The structure that produces egg cells in the flowers and cones of seed-producing plants. After fertilization, an ovule develops into a seed.

Placenta—A temporary organ that connects an embryo to its mother in her uterus during pregnancy. It delivers food and oxygen and removes waste by way of the mother's blood supply.

Pollen—The structure that produces sperm cells in the flowers and cones of seed-producing plants. Pollen grains are carried to the ovules of other plants by the wind or by an animal pollinator.

Reproduction—The process that living things go through to produce offspring. The two types of reproduction are sexual reproduction and asexual reproduction, which are also called crossing and cloning. Some invertebrates and many plants can reproduce both sexually and asexually.

Seed—A plant embryo in an early stage of development. It is packaged with a store of food inside of a protective shell called a seed coat. After a period of rest, the seed is ready to sprout.

Sexual reproduction—See **Crossing**.

Sperm cell—The smaller type of gamete, or reproductive cell. Sperm cells are made by male animals in organs called testes, and plants make sperm cells in the pollen of flowers and cones. Each sperm cell carries a single set of genes and is designed to fuse with an egg cell during fertilization to start a new life.

Testes—The organs that produce sperm cells in male animals.

Trait—A specific feature, or characteristic, of an organism. The traits of a living organism are determined by its genes, the environment, or both.

Uterus—The internal organ in female animals designed to nourish and protect an embryo during development.

Zygote—A fertilized egg that results from a sperm cell fusing with an egg cell during sexual reproduction. It results in a single cell with two sets of genes, and starts the growth of a brand new living thing.

What's in Your Backyard?

I wrote and drew this book about a few of the species that live in my backyard and neighborhood. But the wildlife in your habitat might be completely different. Use your senses to search for clues about which plants and animals are making more near you. Look high and low, listen carefully, and follow your nose. Can you find any of the following things at your school, in a nearby park, or in your own backyard? Take notes or make a drawing to start a field journal of what you discover!

anthills	egg sacs	nests
beehives	eggshells	pollen
berries	flowers	seeds
courtship calls	fruit	spores
eggs	fungi	tree cones

Meiosis Magic

Crossing is when two gametes—an egg cell and a sperm cell—meet and merge during the process of fertilization. The result is a zygote with two sets of genes, one from each parent. But how do males and females, who each have two sets of genes, produce these gametes that have only one set? To find the answer we need to circle back to the beginning and take a closer look at those packages of genes called chromosomes—and their incredible dance moves.

When an animal's body needs to repair a bone, for example, it makes copies of the bone cells that it already has. During this copying process, called mitosis (my-toe-suhs), a cell makes an exact copy of all of its chromosomes. Then the cell divides to make two new identical cells. Mitosis is how an embryo grows into a baby, and how new cells replace old ones in full-grown adults. But unlike other cells in the body, *gametes* are made through a process called meiosis (my-oh-suhs). At first, meiosis starts out just like mitosis—a cell makes an exact copy of all of its chromosomes. But before the cell divides, matching chromosomes pair up for an astonishing dance. As the partners move, they join together . . . *and swap tips*. The traded genes stay in the right order but have been switched to stick with a different chromosome. When the dance partners separate, the cell divides, then divides *again*. This division makes four new gametes that each contain one completely unique set of genes.

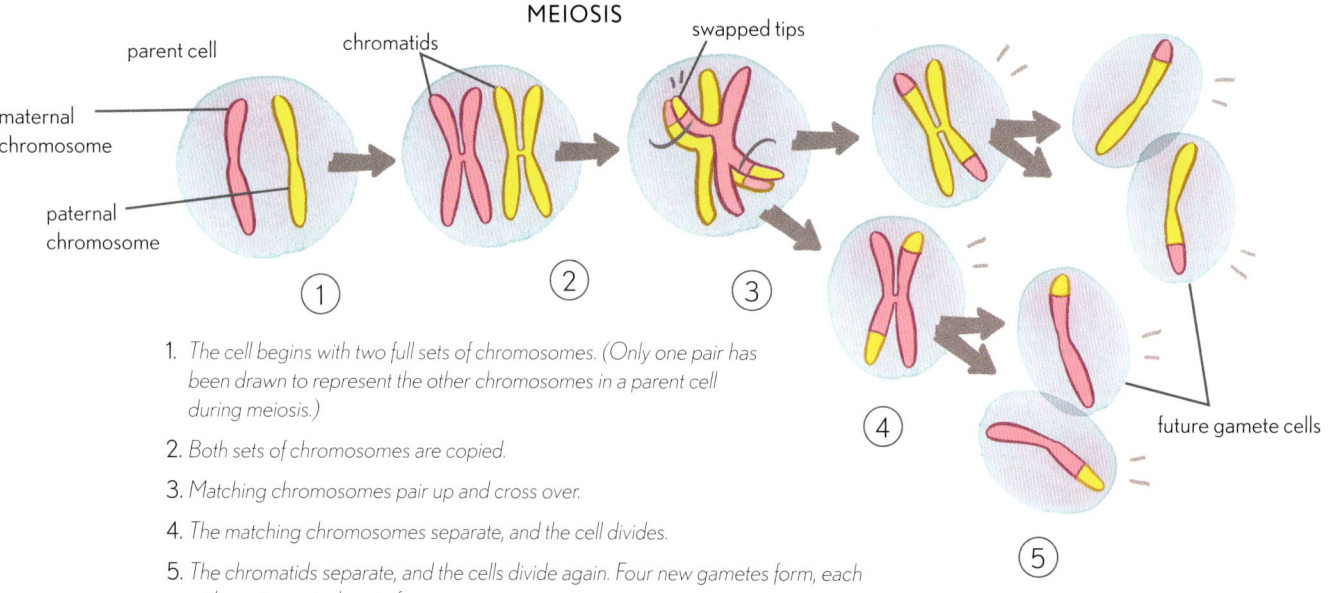

MEIOSIS

parent cell · chromatids · swapped tips · maternal chromosome · paternal chromosome · future gamete cells

1. *The cell begins with two full sets of chromosomes. (Only one pair has been drawn to represent the other chromosomes in a parent cell during meiosis.)*
2. *Both sets of chromosomes are copied.*
3. *Matching chromosomes pair up and cross over.*
4. *The matching chromosomes separate, and the cell divides.*
5. *The chromatids separate, and the cells divide again. Four new gametes form, each with a unique single set of genes.*

Because of this dance—called crossing over—two different sets of genes can be shuffled into a single gamete. It happens all the time in the reproductive organs of living things, and the results are essential to life as we know it. Without meiosis and fertilization, there's little chance of change from one generation to the next. If our ancient ancestors hadn't found a new way to reproduce by crossing instead of cloning, we might all still be single-celled amoeba drifting around on the ocean floor.

A Note from the Author

When it comes to making more, exceptions are everywhere. Life has a dizzying number of ways to reproduce. There are mammals that lay eggs, fish that give birth, and a species of lizard that is entirely female. Viruses evolve and replicate but are not alive, and the sperm cells in one species of fruit fly measure twenty times its body length. Sex determination—who makes eggs, who makes sperm—is anything but easy, and not strictly binary. In most plants and many invertebrates, individuals can make both sperm and eggs at once, though of course "most" living things are actually microbes and reproduce by splitting in two. In turtles, sex is determined by incubation temperature, and in birds it's a chromosome in the *egg* that makes a chick male or female. Reef fish are famous for changing sex on cue, and some species of fungi have over 20,000 different sexual identities. In bees, ants, and wasps, drones have grandfathers but not fathers—males are produced from a queen's *unfertilized* eggs and have only one set of genes.

In our own species, too, there are lots of exceptions, and families are made in all sorts of different ways. Human egg cells can be fertilized in a petri dish, infants can arrive by C-section, children can be adopted by new parents, and adults can choose who they love and how they are seen. For what I've left out, for what isn't here, biologists, parents, critical readers everywhere, please forgive me. There is much, much more to this story, but that's not the work of this book. This book is meant to be a tool for adults and children, and a love letter to the natural world. I also hope that it can help pave the way for the (harder) human conversations about love and intimacy on the road ahead. Most of our country's children don't grow up raising chickens and delivering lambs, and so they have lots of questions about the way it all works. *How does a baby get out of its mom? Why are those bugs stuck together?* The truth is simple—that every living thing has parents—and that we all get our start as a single cell. From something known comes something *new*. What a breathtaking history we share with all of life on Earth.

This book was conceived before I became a parent and it was delivered to the publisher during a global pandemic. The successive variants of COVID-19 have been a real-time lesson in selection and change, and as our planet heats up, more changes are coming. Life is ever evolving, and life finds a way—there will be evolutionary winners on a warmer planet, too. But as humans we are uniquely conscious and capable, and it falls to us to be good stewards to the other species on this ship. Like them, we are made of stardust, and carry within our cells a billion years of crossing and change. To paraphrase the biologist E. O. Wilson, life has swallowed the storms and folded them into our genes, one generation at a time. Making more is why there are flowers and bird song, why fruit is sweet, why we see sunsets in color. It has transformed a watery, silent rock into the vibrant world we know and love, and I, for one, am grateful to be here. Look at us, we're amazing! Every one of us—unique! We can sing, we can dance, we can draw, we can build, and yes—we can even make more.

Acknowledgments

From the first idea to the final pages, this project has been nearly a decade in the making. It's taken a small village to bring this book into the world and I am deeply grateful to the following people.

To my editor, Simon Boughton, who once again has proven himself to be one of the best in children's publishing—curious, instinctive, deeply patient, and always reassuring. I am forever thankful to him for taking a chance on this pitch while keeping any doubts to himself, and for applying just the right mix of time and pressure for the book to evolve as it needed. To Stephen Barr, my dear friend and agent, for his optimism, insight, curiosity, and enduring diligence. He has championed this book at every step since my first excited ramblings, and without his fearless endorsement and sustaining discussions, this project would still be an idea in my head. To the team of wonderful folks at W. W. Norton, who did the hard work of transforming a pile of files into a bound book—it's finally real! I am especially grateful to Hana Anouk Nakamura for her direction and Angela Corbo Gier for her gorgeous design, and to Julia Druskin, Mike van Mantgem, and Jessica Murphy for their careful attention.

To the cast of brilliant biologists, botanists, ecologists, veterinarians, and zoologists who I consulted as this book slowly developed, who were so generous with their time, ideas, direction, and feedback: Bruce Dugger, Tiffany Garcia, Guillermo Giannico, Sarah Kincaid, Bruce McCune, Anne Mary Myers, Deanna H. Olson, Greg Reed, and Brad Smith. I am especially indebted to Lindsay Adrean, Jamie Cornelius, Sam Leiboff, David Maddison, Robert Mason, Amanda Nahlik, and Karen Timm for their key advice, precision criticism, reference materials, and unwavering enthusiasm. They saved me from myself on several occasions. Any remaining errors are my own.

To my parents, Linda and Jean-Claude, my brother Steven, and my sisters in spirit, Kristi Schramm, Karen Shaw, and Brie Spells, for the gift of their love and their relentless willingness to track down resources or weigh in on a sentence or a sketch at a moment's notice. To my colleagues in publishing, Elisha Cooper, Brian Floca, Richard Ho, R. Kikuo Johnson, David Macaulay, Barb Rosenstock, Sarah Stewart Taylor, Maris Wicks, and especially Jessica Lanan, for their wise counsel and friendship. To the many librarians, teachers, and parents I reached out to as the manuscript took shape, especially Marissa Goodell, Christine Gough, Elizabeth Johnson, and Steph and Mike McHugh, for their thoughtful praise and worthy criticism. To the students who bravely raised their hands during my author visits to ask how sharks make babies and how elephants are born, I hope this is the book you've been looking for. To my incredible friends who cheered me on—especially Emily Stewart, Johanna Tower, and Janet Yousey—and to my neighbors who kindly suggested resources and shared their photos of our local fauna.

To the outdoor wildlife in my backyard in western Oregon, the deer and ferns and hummingbirds, for their beauty in every season. To the indoor wildlife, Jackson and Tristan, for buoying me with their joy and reminding me of what's most important. And lastly—but really first and most of all—to Tim Stout, who made breakfast, played with the kids, and kept our life going for the months (and years) it took to write and draw this book bird by snake by squirrel. He's the best friend, collaborator, husband, and father I could ever possibly imagine, and I am beyond grateful that his faith never wavered in this project even when my own was long gone. I love you, Tim—thanks for picking me. PS, our genes go great together.

SELECTED SOURCES

I consulted hundreds of books, scientific journals, websites, documentaries, and my own wildlife photos and videos as I wrote and drew this book. Some of the most broadly helpful sources were the following. For a suggested reading list and a more complete list of my sources, please visit **katherineroy.com**.

BOOKS

Forsyth, Adrian. *A Natural History of Sex: The Ecology and Evolution of Mating Behavior.* Firefly Books, 2001.

Judson, Olivia. *Dr. Tatiana's Sex Advice to All Creation.* Henry Holt and Company, 2002.

King, A. S., and J. McLelland. *Birds: Their Structure and Function*, 2nd ed. W. B. Saunders, 1983.

Lane, Nick. *Life Ascending: The Ten Great Inventions of Evolution.* W. W. Norton, 2009.

Mauseth, James D. *Botany: An Introduction to Plant Biology*, 2nd ed. Jones and Bartlett Publishers, 1998.

Milton, Hildebrand. *Analysis of Vertebrate Structure*, 4th ed. Wiley, 1994.

Noden, Drew M., and Alexander DeLahunta. *The Embryology of Domestic Animals: Developmental Mechanisms and Malformations.* Williams and Wilkins, 1985.

Reece, Jane B., et al. *Campbell Biology*, 10th ed. Pearson Education, 2014.

Schultz, Mark. *The Stuff of Life: A Graphic Guide to Genetics and DNA.* Hill and Wang, 2009.

Shubin, Neil. *Your Inner Fish: A Journey into the 3.5-Billion-Year History of the Human Body.* Vintage Books, 2009.

For information about permission to reproduce selections
from this book, write to
Permissions, W. W. Norton & Company, Inc.,
500 Fifth Avenue, New York, NY 10110

For information about special discounts
for bulk purchases, please contact
W. W. Norton Special Sales at
specialsales@wwnorton.com or 800-233-4830

Manufacturing by Toppan Leefung
Book design by Hana Anouk Nakamura and Angela Corbo Gier
Production manager: Julia Druskin

ISBN 978-1-324-01584-0

W. W. Norton & Company, Inc., 500 Fifth Avenue, New York, N.Y. 10110
www.wwnorton.com
W. W. Norton & Company Ltd., 15 Carlisle Street, London W1D 3BS

1 2 3 4 5 6 7 8 9 0